Frank,
Hope you
...

Cocktail Waitress Wisdom

*Life lessons learned while
carrying a tray in Las Vegas*

By
Heidi Harris

Published in Las Vegas, Nevada, by Heidiology Enterprises

Design and Artwork by Deena Ippolito
Photography by Rocky Nash

Heidiology Enterprises
840 S. Rancho Dr. Ste 4-555
Las Vegas, NV 89106

ISBN: 0-982983506

Printed in the United States of America

This book is dedicated to all the cocktail waitresses who are overworked, under-appreciated, and far too often, underestimated.

Special thanks to all the girls I worked with over the years who graciously resisted the urge to kill me while I tried to grow up.

Cocktail Waitress
Wisdom:

Table of Contents

Chapter		Page

Introduction

I worked as a cocktail waitress in Las Vegas casinos for over ten years. You might think it's a mindless job that any bimbo with high heels and breast implants can do, but you'd be wrong. Doing the job well requires speed, organizational skills and more than a little tolerance for the (often ungrateful) public.

Over the years, and the thousands of drinks I served, I learned a lot about people, and a lot about life. I call it Cocktail Waitress Wisdom, and I hope some of the lessons I learned will "serve" you well.

It Ain't All About You

One of the first lessons I learned as a fresh faced 21-year-old casino cocktail waitress was *that it ain't all about you.*

When someone is rude to you at work, or shows up in a foul mood, it's easy to take it personally if you're young and sensitive. (I was THEN – that would change).

One day when I was fairly new, a girl was really being rude to me for no reason, and I figured it had to be my fault. Even though I have a unique talent for ticking off anyone, sooner or later, up to that point, she and I had never argued, so I couldn't figure it out.

It was only when I mentioned it to my bartender that I found out what was wrong…"that's because she put her rent money in the slot machines last night". Oh, now I get it. I would see that movie a lot in the years to come.

No matter where you work, you're going to run into people who are having bad days, for whatever reason. Once you realize it ain't all about you, and you're not responsible for anyone else's mood, you'll be better off.

Nowadays, unless I have personally done something worthy of an apology, I no longer take crabby behavior personally. And besides, I can be pretty crabby myself – ask anyone!

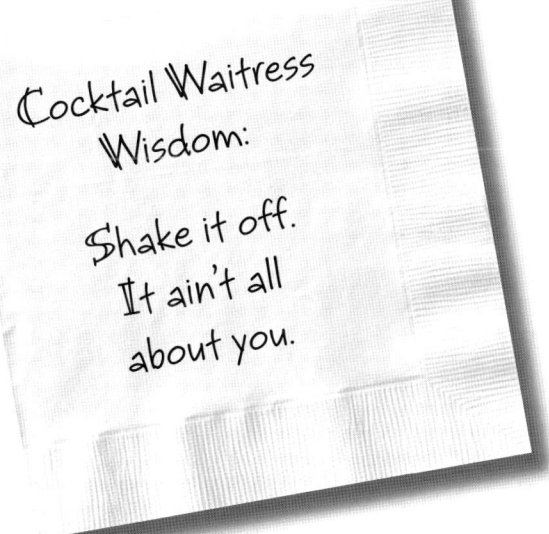

Cocktail Waitress
Wisdom:

Shake it off.
It ain't all
about you.

Every day has to be a new day

When you "do" cocktails (the term) for a living, you are required to work in a very small space with people you may or may not like.

Most service bars are very small, often with three or more girls working in them, in addition to a bartender, bar back, bar porter, etc. There's no way to avoid each other, even if you want to.

There's a symbiotic relationship between the server and the bartender. Since you're giving them a percentage of your tips, they are counting on you to get the maximum number of drinks out per shift. Even if they hate your guts, it's in their best interest to get your order poured quickly, if for no other reason than to get you out of the service bar for a few minutes!

For this reason, every day HAS to be a new day. Even if you wanted to kill the girl who works the Sports Book yesterday, you HAVE to get along today, because you'll be literally rubbing elbows with her all day. There's no slamming an office door. Although it can be painful to have to stare at someone you may not like all day, or do sidework next to her, you're stuck.

This approach will serve you well in any workplace. Even if you do have an office door you can close, you'll run into that person in meetings, at parties, or maybe another job down the road. You don't have to invite them over for dinner, but you'd better be professional. It never hurts.

Years after I left cocktails, a girl I worked with came up to my desk at my new job, all huffy because another woman had passed her in the hall and not said hello! It was all I could do not to laugh out loud.

A dose of Cocktail Waitress Wisdom would have served her well. Grow up! Get over it. Save your huff for something important.

Don't try to befriend
everyone at work

Sometimes the most you can hope for is grudging respect from your co-workers. Sarah Palin wasn't the first to earn the nickname "barracuda". Most of ones I know wear high heels and carry trays.

The first cocktail job I had, in a total dive bar in Tucson, when I was only 19, (the legal drinking age then) was an eye opener.

I worked with a very big Native American girl named Mary, who would drink all night while serving (it was allowed) and loudly lay claim to any dollar bill that was found on the floor as we swept up at night! She would literally knock you over at the bar. Needless to say, it was a horrible job. Then, to top it off, when they fired me (guess I didn't fit in), the boss came over to bring my final check, and tried to get me in bed!!! I was growing up fast. (Luckily, he was the only boss who ever tried that)

Over the years, I worked with many people who were very damaged. Sadly, many of the girls had such horrible backgrounds that in some cases, they barely spoke to their own adult children. And you can imagine the divorce rate. Drugs and drinking on the job were often a problem, not just for the people who used, but for the rest of us, who had to try to bob and weave around them all day. Some days it was the best show in town!

Frankly, cocktail waitressing tends to attract a lot of irresponsible people. You don't need to wait until payday to buy things, since you always have tip money, and if you blow all of it in the poker machines after work, you'll have cash again tomorrow.

But don't think the girls were all vapid. Far from it. I attended college while I worked in a casino, and so did some of the other girls. The reality is, in Vegas, you can often make more money serving drinks than you can using your degree. Sad, but true. Education is never wasted, but common sense and street smarts will often get you a lot further in life.

Wherever you work, you will have to deal with people who are damaged or just plain mean. All you can do is try to show compassion for those who've been through a lot, and stand up for yourself when necessary.

Cocktail Waitress
Wisdom:

Don't waste your time
trying to befriend
people who don't
even like themselves.

Watch what you say, it may come back to bite you...or benefit you!

Gossip is always a bad idea, and since alliances are fluid at best in any work setting, it usually comes back to bite you. Remember, once it's out of your mouth, it's out of your hands

Here's a perfect illustration of where things could have gone really wrong. When I first started at the Las Vegas casino where I would spend the next ten years, there was a girl named "Susie" who was an old battle ax with no patience for the new girls. She would literally push you out of the way if you were taking too long.

She successfully intimidated all the new girls, especially me.

I was still trying to figure out how to survive the shift each day, when I ran into a former co-worker at the mall. She asked how the new job was going, and I told her it was great. She asked if I knew a girl named "Susie". Hmmm...what to say?

I smiled through gritted teeth and answered (truthfully), "You know, she's a great cocktail waitress." It was true, she WAS lightning fast and efficient - I just left the wicked witch part out.

It so happened that my former co-worker was dating "Susie's" brother, so word got back, as it always does. And from that day on, the atmosphere at work changed completely, at least for me.

Wise words (and uncharacteristic restraint on my part) had served me well.

Cocktail Waitress
Wisdom:

"When in doubt,
leave it out!"

Cocktail Waitress
Wisdom:

"Miranda Rule":
Anything you say can
and will be used
against you"

The nickel player mentality

Something you will see very quickly in the casino is what I have termed the "nickel player mentality."

The cheapest people are the most demanding. Always.

In the casino business, we cocktail waitresses learn pretty fast that the nickel slots are the worst place to work. (With the possible exception of Bingo. I could never take those crabby old ladies)

If you're going to work slots, dollar slots are the way to go, but when you walk through them, you can almost hear your pantyhose run, it's so quiet. You have to practically beg them to drink.

Walk through nickels, and it's like a revival meeting! Everyone's waving their arms like they've been stranded on a desert island, and they all want two drinks apiece, "and can you blend my Orange Julius™ with whipped cream and an extra cherry?"

Someday I'm going to find the cocktail waitress who started that Julius nonsense. And kill her. Slowly.

What will you get for all your trouble?

Maybe a few nickels. More likely nothing at all! You work four times as hard and make less money.

Whether you're in marketing, retail, or real estate, you've seen this time and again. I can't explain it, but it's the case in every business. The less they have (or want) to spend, the more they expect, or demand. Go figure.

And if you're a nickel player, my apologies…but you know I'm telling the truth.

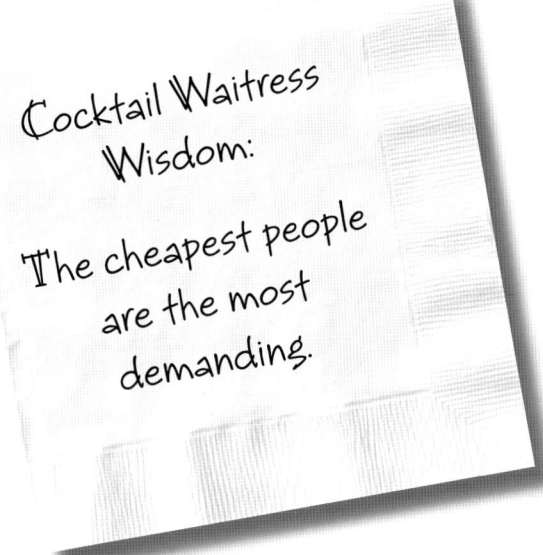

Cocktail Waitress
Wisdom:

The cheapest people
are the most
demanding.

The customer is NOT always right (despite what the employee manual says)

Anyone who's worked in customer service knows this.

Personally, I could never wait on the public again without a Prozac™ drip. I have learned that you can't reason with rude people, and I've also been disgusted by some of the things I've seen customers do.

On one occasion, a couple brought their adult son, who was in a wheelchair, to the casino. He didn't appear to be able to move anything other than his head.

They ordered drinks, and when I came back and started to put them down, the "paralyzed" son raised his arm and karate chopped my tray, pulling all its contents into his lap, including hot coffee!

I was mortified, and ran to the bar to get towels. I warned the other girls about him, but didn't bother to notify my boss. I should have.

Wanna guess what happened? Naturally the parents tried to sue the casino, claiming I had dumped my tray on him! They claimed he couldn't lift up his arms, but when the security officer was taking a report, he did just that!
I was covered legally, because I had told

the other girls at the time what had happened, and to watch out for him. The next time I saw them in the casino, they had tied his arms down to the wheelchair. Very sad. Just goes to show you…

I never had the patience some of the other girls did, and one day I asked a girl who had a particularly hectic station about it. "Why don't you ever get frustrated with the customers?" She answered matter of factly, "That's why I drink all day." She would just sip wine all day long throughout her shift.

Sadly, that girl's lifestyle caught up with her, and she died in her 30's.

For the record, management did not condone drinking on the job, but they know it goes on, so that's why most service bars don't carry real Bailey's™ Irish Cream…too many employees drink it in their coffee. They only stock the generic brands.

As for me, I had learned long ago in that bar in Tucson where drinking on the job was allowed (after I tried it one night) that I cannot drink and work. And since I don't do other drugs, I was stuck being the sober, sometimes crabby one.

Sometimes drastic action is called for. One night, a girl working the 21 pit had a guy stick his hand right into her uniform top! She cold-cocked him with her tray, and knocked him right off the stool.

I always liked that girl…

Of course, there was always the danger of some crazy customer following you to your car, knowing you're carrying cash. A girl I worked with was walking to her car after working swing shift one night, and a guy pulled a gun on her in the parking lot, forcing her into her car.

She was wise enough to know that she had no chance if he took her somewhere else. So with one hand, she threw her car keys out the window, and as she did, she put her other hand over the muzzle of the gun. The guy actually fired right through her hand, and ran off, but she recovered fully. Gutsy!

Cocktail waitressing makes you street smart, and that's never a bad thing.

Cocktail Waitress Wisdom:

The customer is NOT always right.

Cocktail Waitress Wisdom:

street smarts are better than book smarts

No one has the right to denigrate you, regardless of your job title or uniform

When you "do" cocktails for a few years, you'll learn that you need a snappy comeback for a variety of situations.

People will say some pretty rude things to you based on the fact that you're not wearing much. However, last time I checked, cocktail waitressing was a legal occupation. You don't have the right to talk down to me because I'm wearing fishnets.

One day, I was in the service bar, which was open to the bar area, where customers sat. I was complaining about something to the other girls (imagine that). And a customer at the bar, who had never met me, said, "What's the matter, didn't you get any last night"?

I shot him the look of death and said, "How dare you speak to me that way just because I'm wearing a short dress? How would you like it if someone spoke to your wife or daughter like that?"

I said a lot more than that, but you get the picture. When I tell you that he literally slithered off his barstool, I'm not kidding. Sometimes you have to teach men what their mamas should have. It's never too late, and you'll do the sisterhood a favor.

Cocktail Waitress
Wisdom:

Sometimes you have to
teach men what their
mamas didn't.

Harmless banter vs. real sexual harassment – grow up and recognize the difference

I have a tough time understanding women who cry sexual harassment every time some guy says, "You look nice today." Really? Grow up and see the difference. For my money, unless a boss says, "Sleep with me or you're fired," anything else can be handled by YOU.

Whenever you have men and women working together, there's bound to be sexual banter, especially in a bar. I realize that not everyone is a natural smart ass like I am (can you tell?), but whether you're in the boardroom or the barroom, handling things in a fun, friendly way will serve you well.

I have done this numerous times, and so has every other girl with a tray. It's called being a Big Girl. Besides the fact that once you've filed a sexual harassment lawsuit, you're marked for good, it's just better to handle these things yourself.

For example, my bartender came in one day and said, "I had a dream about you last night." Rather than get all huffy, I said, "Yeah, how much do you owe me?" We both laughed, and the workday had begun. He wasn't hitting on me; it was just harmless banter. Another time, a high level manager walked into the service bar, looked me up and down, and said, "You need to put on some weight." I looked HIM up and down and said, "Yeah, how about 195 pounds, right now?" He laughed and said, "That's a good one!"

Sexual harassment? Not! He was happily married (then) and once again, his comments were harmless. If you show the men at work that you can handle it with a sense of humor, and come right back at 'em, you'll have a lot more fun. Lighten up.

Sometimes you are forced to draw the line. I worked for years in the poker room with a guy who was happily married, but a bit of a joker. One day, I had a tray full of drinks, and as I was attempting to squeeze between two poker tables and behind him (he was waiting to sit down and deal), he stuck his hand out and practically forced me to scrape my crotch across his hand, because I had no room to maneuver around him.

Boy, was I ticked off! I was so mad, I was shaking. I liked Jim, and he really wasn't trying to hit on me, just clowning around, but this crossed the line.

Instead of running to the boss, like a Little Girl, I went home and calmed down, and plotted my strategy.

The next day, much calmer, I caught him alone in the back of the poker room. I told him, "I'm only gonna say this once. If you ever do that again, I'm going to dump my entire tray, hot, cold, sticky or otherwise, all over you, and then YOU can explain to the Poker Room Manager why you can't go in the "box" (dealer's seat)!" He tried to speak, but I shut him down. I told him I wasn't going to the boss, I was handling it myself, and those were the rules.

He actually behaved for quite some time after that, until one day he came to work with one of those fake arms that people hang outside of their car trunk. He started toward me with it, and I had a bottle of milk in my hand. I poured the milk all over his arm, reminded him of what I had said, and that was the end of it.

We are still friends to this day. Had I gone to the boss, I would have proven that I was a 25 year-old crybaby, and the whole casino would have heard about it. And what would have been accomplished? More than I accomplished myself? I think not.

Remember that YOU teach people what you will or won't tolerate, and how you want to be viewed. Do you want to be treated with respect? Or be branded a baby or a bitch? You decide.

Your daddy can't go to work with his little girl every day, so grow up, apply a little Cocktail Waitress Wisdom, and you'll be fine.

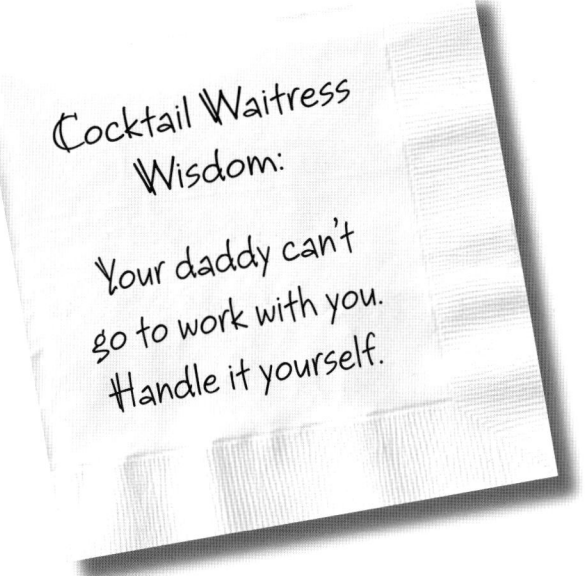

Cocktail Waitress Wisdom:

Your daddy can't go to work with you. Handle it yourself.

So ya wanna be a Cocktail Waitress?

Pros

• Reasonably good money, considering there's no formal education required.

• No responsibilities beyond your shift. No work related e-mails to answer, boring meetings to attend, or calls on your days off.

• You'll get some exercise while you work.

• You'll learn a lot about life and people.

Cons

• Dealing with the drinking, gambling public can harden you in ways you may not expect.

• The money doesn't get better. It can be deceiving when you're young, when $100 a day sounds like great money. The reality is, tips have been stagnant for years. For the most part, people are still tipping the same amount they were 30 years ago. Ask a valet parker. Too many people still give them $1! And of course, some still think "Tipping" is a city in China.

• If you have a weakness for drugs and/or gambling, it's a job that can destroy you. I've seen it happen too many times.

• Divorce is rampant, mainly because girls suddenly become self-supporting, and don't feel the need to work on their marriages. And because many of the other girls badmouth their boyfriends and husbands all day, it can be a poisonous environment if you're not grounded.

• Secondhand smoke is an issue, although my lungs are fine after all the years I spent in the casino. And the casinos have much better air filtration than they used to.

- You can't do it forever, because your body will eventually betray you. And you'll look silly in that skimpy outfit. You have to think about what you're going to do next.

Bottom line:
Cocktail waitressing is like any other job. If you make the best of it, you'll do fine. Save your money and buy a home, go to school, travel, and otherwise better your life.

But…if you have an out of wedlock baby with some bum, pick up a video poker or drug habit, or neglect to plan for the future, you'll be trapped, and maybe wind up a Vegas Cocktailasaurus…!

No matter what you do for a living, apply a little Cocktail Waitress Wisdom, and you'll be fine.